Praise for *A Testament of Devotion*

"There is spiritual power between the covers of this beautiful book! I first read *A Testament of Devotion* as a young seminary student twenty years ago, and it so touched my spiritually hungry heart that it has remained within an arm's reach ever since. The reading of Thomas Kelly's little volume should not be a mere option for those on the inward path of spiritual growth, it should be a requirement. Advice to the reader: Beware—your life may be transformed!"

—JAMES R. NEWBY
editor of *Quaker Life* magazine

"America, however wonderful its amusement parks and shopping malls, is not a congenial place for becoming a saint. But Thomas Kelly did it, ranking high among those who lived well in bad times. His *Testament of Devotion* gives witness to a holy life lived in the noise and density of American traffic. In a land as spare in saints as ours, we cannot afford to neglect a single one."

—EUGENE H. PETERSON
author of *Answering God* and *Reversed Thunder*

"This classic treasure is a deep well to which I am forever returning. It deserves to endure. I highly recommend it."

—MACRINA WIEDERKEHR
author of *A Tree Full of Angels*

"If you want to find the places in your soul where God awaits you, *A Testament of Devotion* will show you the way. For contemporary people—living in highrises, working in skyscrapers, immersed in the network of world-wide communications—Kelly imparts age-old insights into the practicalities of walking through life with Jesus. You have only to try them to find them true."

—DALLAS WILLARD
author of *The Spirit of the Disciplines*

A Testament of
Devotion

A Testament of
Devotion

Thomas R. Kelly

HarperSanFrancisco
A Division of HarperCollins*Publishers*

LIBRARY OF CONGRESS CATALOGING-IN-PUBLICATION DATA

Kelly, Thomas R. (Thomas Raymond), 1893–1941.
A testament of devotion / Thomas R. Kelly.
    p.   cm.
Originally published: New York : Harper, c1941.
ISBN 0-06-064212-2 (alk. paper)
1. Devotional literature.   2. Society of Friends.
    3. Large type books.
    I. Title.
BV4832.K43 1992   91-55339
248.4' 896—dc20   CIP

91 92 93 94 95 ❖ K P 10 9 8 7 6 5 4 3 2 1

This edition is printed on acid-free paper that meets the American National Standards Institute Z39.48 Standard.

CONTENTS

INTRODUCTION

I still remember my first encounter with *A Testament of Devotion* many years ago. It was a cold, rainy February morning, and I had just slumped into a chair at the Dulles International Airport to wait for my flight. Exhausted from a hectic schedule of "muchness" and "manyness," I was glad for the solitude of airport and airplane as I made the trek from D.C. to L.A.

I pulled out the slender volume I had brought along for reading during free moments. Immediately Thomas Kelly caught my attention by describing perfectly my condition and the condition of so many I knew: "We feel honestly the pull of many obligations and try to fulfill them all. And we are unhappy, uneasy, strained, oppressed, and fearful we shall be shallow." Yes, I had to confess I saw myself in those words. To all who knew me I was confident and in command, but inwardly I was tired and scattered.

Then my eyes came upon words of hope and promise: "We have hints that there is a way of life vastly richer and deeper than all this hurried existence, a life of unhurried serenity and peace and power. If only we could slip over into that Center!" Instinctively, I know that he was speaking of a reality beyond my experience. Please understand me, I was not ungodly or irreverent—just the opposite. My problem was that I was so serious, so concerned to do what was right, that I felt compelled to respond to every call to service. After all, they *were* wonderful opportunities to minister in Christ's name. The end result, however, was what Kelly describes as "an intolerable scramble of panting feverishness."

Then came the sentence that was to prompt an inner revolution: "We have seen and known some people who seem to have found this deep Center of living, where the fretful calls of life are integrated, where no as well as yes can be said with confidence." I knew I had been found out. This ability to say yes and no out of "the divine Center," as Kelly calls it, was foreign to me. Oh, I could say yes easily enough, because opportunities to serve carried an aura of spirituality and sacrifice. But to say no was another matter altogether. What would people think of me if I refused?

Even in that congested airport terminal I was utterly alone with the Alone. The cold rain splattering on the window was matched by the hot tears splattering on my jacket. The chair where I sat was a holy place, an altar. I was never to be the same. Quietly, I asked God to give me the ability to say no when it was right and good.

Back home, I was once again caught up in a flurry of activity. But I had made one decision: Friday nights were to be reserved for the family. It was a small decision at the time; nobody but I knew about it. I shared it with my wife Carolynn and the boys in a casual, offhand fashion; they did not know that it was a covenant commitment, a crossroads decision. Nor did I, really. It just seemed like the right thing to do—hardly what you would call a God-given directive.

But then the phone call came. It was a denominational executive. Would I be willing to speak to such-and-such a group next Friday night? There it was, another wonderful opportunity. Almost without thinking I blurted out, "Oh, no, I can't." The response was measured. "Oh, do you have another commitment?" I felt trapped. (In those days I did not know that I could quite legitimately say that I did indeed have a very important commitment.) Cautiously but purposefully, I answered simply, "No," with no attempt to justify or explain my decision. There followed what seemed like an eternity of silence. I could almost feel the condemnation traveling through the telephone wires. I knew I had made a decision that made me seem less dedicated to someone for whom I genuinely cared. After a moment we shared a few pleasantries and then hung up.

But as the phone hit the receiver I jumped out of my chair shouting, "Hallelujah!" I had yielded to the Center, and the result was electrifying. That simple no coming out of divine promptings set me free from the tyranny of others. Even more, it set me free from my own inner clamoring for attention and recognition and applause.

This incident is so small and insignificant that it is almost embarrassing to relate it to you. I'm sure my

4

denominational friend does not even recall the phone conversation. And yet I had turned a corner. Even now I sometimes wish that something terribly important precipitated such an inner transformation. But there it is, a trivial event, yet it changed everything for me. Perhaps it has been that way for you also. At least I know that often the genuinely significant issues are decided in the small corners of life. And one of the greatest gifts that Thomas Kelly brings to us is an ability to see the Holy in the most common of places and the most unexpected of events.

Since that first day in a Washington, D.C. airport, I have returned often to *A Testament of Devotion*. Each time I leaf through its pages, pausing at well-marked passages, I know I am in the presence of a giant soul. I am the better for the encounter. I'm sure you will be too.

Richard J. Foster
OCTOBER 1991

THE LIGHT WITHIN

Meister Eckhart wrote, "As thou art in church or cell, that same frame of mind carry out into the world, into its turmoil and its fitfulness." Deep within us all there is an amazing inner sanctuary of the soul, a holy place, a Divine Center, a speaking Voice, to which we may continually return. Eternity is at our hearts, pressing upon our time-torn lives, warming us with intimations of an astounding destiny, calling us home unto Itself. Yielding to these persuasions, gladly committing ourselves in body and soul, utterly and completely, to the Light Within, is the beginning of true life. It is a dynamic center, a creative Life that presses to birth within us. It is a Light Within that illumines the face of God and casts new shadows and new glories upon the human face. It is a seed stirring to life if we do not choke it. It is the Shekinah of the soul, the Presence in the midst. Here is the Slumbering

Christ, stirring to be awakened, to become the soul we clothe in earthly form and action. And He is within us all.

You who read these words already know this inner Life and Light. For by this very Light within you is your recognition given. In this humanistic age we suppose we are the initiators and God is the responder. But the Living Christ within us is the initiator, and we are the responders. God the Lover, the accuser, the revealer of light and darkness presses within us. "Behold I stand at the door and knock." And all our apparent initiative is already a response, a testimonial to His secret presence and working within us.

The basic response of the soul to the Light is internal adoration and joy, thanksgiving and worship, self-surrender and listening. The secret places of the heart cease to be our noisy workshop. They become a holy sanctuary of adoration and of self-oblation, where we are kept in perfect peace, if our minds be stayed on Him who has found us in the inward springs of our life. And in brief intervals of overpowering visitation we are able to carry the sanctuary frame of mind out into the world, into its turmoil and its fitfulness, and in a hyperesthesia of the soul, we see all humankind tinged with deeper shadows and touched with Galilean glories. Powerfully are the springs of our will moved to an abandon of singing love toward God; powerfully are we moved to a new and over-coming love toward time-blinded human beings and all creation. In this Center of Creation all things are ours, and we are Christ's and Christ is God's. We are owned beings, ready to run and not be weary and to walk and not faint.

But the light fades, the will weakens, the humdrum returns. Can we stay this fading? No; nor should we try, for we must learn the disciplines of His will.

The Inner Light, the Inward Christ, is no mere doctrine, belonging peculiarly to a small religious fellowship, to be accepted or rejected as a mere belief. It is the living Center of Reference for all Christian souls and Christian groups—yes, and of non-Christian groups as well—who seriously mean to dwell in the secret place of the Most High. He is the center and source of action, not the endpoint of thought. He is the locus of commitment, not a problem for debate. Practice comes first in religion, not theory or dogma.

And Christian practice is not exhausted in outward deeds. These are the fruits, not the roots. A practicing Christian must above all be one who practices the perpetual return of the soul into the inner sanctuary, who brings the world into its Light and rejudges it, who brings the Light into the world with all its turmoil and its fitfulness and re-creates it (after the pattern seen on the Mount). To the reverent exploration of this practice we now address ourselves.

II

There is a way of ordering our mental life on more than one level at once. On one level we may be thinking, discussing, seeing, calculating, meeting all the demands of external affairs. But deep within, behind the scenes, at a profounder level, we may also be in prayer and adoration, song and worship and a gentle receptiveness to divine breathings.

The secular world of today values and cultivates only the first level, assured that *there* is where the real business of humankind is done, and scorns or smiles in tolerant amusement at the cultivation of the second level—a luxury enterprise, a vestige of superstition, an occupation for special temperaments. But in a deeply religious culture people know that the deep level of prayer and of divine attendance is the most important thing in the world. It is at this deep level that the real business of life is determined. The secular mind is an abbreviated, fragmentary mind, building only upon a part of human nature and neglecting a part—the most glorious part—of a human being's nature, powers, and resources. The religious mind involves the whole person, embraces his or her relations with time within their true ground and setting in the Eternal Lover. It ever keeps close to the fountains of divine creativity. In lowliness it knows joys and stabilities, peace and assurances, that are utterly incomprehensible to the secular mind. It lives in resources and powers that make individuals radiant and triumphant, groups tolerant and bonded together in mutual concern, and is bestirred to an outward life of unremitting labor.

Between the two levels is fruitful interplay, but ever the accent must be upon the deeper level, where the soul ever dwells in the presence of the Holy One. For the religious person is forever bringing all affairs of the first level down into the Light, holding them there in the Presence, reseeing them and the whole of the world of people and things in a new and over-turning way, and responding to them in spontaneous, incisive, and simple ways of love and faith. Facts remain facts when brought into the Presence in the deeper level, but their value, their significance, is wholly realigned. Much apparent wheat becomes utter chaff, and some chaff becomes wheat. Imposing powers? They are out of the Life, and must crumble. Lost causes? If God be for them, who can be against them? Rationally plausible futures? They are weak-ened or certified in the dynamic Life and Light. Tragic suffering? Already He is there, and we actively move, in His tenderness, toward the sufferers. Hopeless debauchees? These are children of God, His concern and ours. Inexorable laws of nature? The dependable framework for divine reconstruction. The fall of a sparrow? The Father's love. For faith and hope and love for all things are engendered in the soul, as we practice their submission and our own to the Light Within, as we humbly see all things, even darkly and as through a glass, yet through the eye of God.

How, then, shall we lay hold of that Life and Power, and live the life of prayer without ceasing? By quiet, persistent practice in turning of all our being, day and night, in prayer and inward worship and surrender, toward Him who calls in the deeps of our souls. Mental habits of inward orientation must be established.

The first days and weeks and months are awkward and painful, but enormously rewarding. Awkward, because it takes constant vigilance and effort and reassertions of the will at the first level. Painful, because our lapses are so frequent, the intervals when we forget Him so long. Rewarding, because we have begun to live.

At first the practice of inward prayer is a process of alternation of attention between outer things and the Inner Light. Preoccupation with either brings the loss of the other. Yet what is sought is not alternation, but simultaneity, worship undergirding every moment, living prayer, the continuous current and background of all moments of life. For sole preoccupation with the world is sleep, but immersion in Him is life. We cease trying to make ourselves the dictators and God the listener, and become the joyful listeners to Him, the Master who does all things well.

There is then no need for fret when faithfully turning to Him if He leads us but slowly into His secret chambers. If He gives us increasing steadiness in the deeper sense of His Presence, we can only quietly thank Him. If He holds us in the stage of alternation, we can thank Him for His loving wisdom and wait upon His guidance through the stages for which we are prepared. For we cannot take Him by storm. The strong adult must become the little child, not understanding but trusting the Father.

But to some at least He gives an amazing stayedness in Him, a well-nigh unbroken life of humble, quiet adoration in His Presence, in the depths of our being. Day and night, winter and summer, sunshine and shadow, He is here, the great Champion. And we are with Him, held in His Tenderness, quickened into quietness and peace, children in Paradise before the Fall, walking with Him in the garden in the heat as well as the cool of the day. Here is not ecstasy but serenity, unshakableness, firmness of life-orientation.

We may suppose these depths of prayer are our achievement, the precipitate of our own habits at the surface level settled into subconscious regions. But this humanistic account misses the autonomy of the life of prayer. It misses the fact that this inner level has a life of its own, invigorated not by us but by a divine Source. There come times when prayer pours forth in volumes and originality such as we cannot create. It rolls through us like a mighty tide. Our prayers are mingled with a vaster Word, a Word that at one time was made flesh. We pray, and yet it is not we who pray, but a Greater who prays in us. Something of our punctiform selfhood is weakened, but never lost. All we can say is, Prayer is taking place, and I am given to be in the orbit. In holy hush we bow in Eternity, and know the Divine Concern tenderly enwrapping us and all things within His persuading love. Here all human initiative has passed into acquiescence, and He works and prays and seeks His own through us, in exquisite, energizing life. Here the autonomy of the inner life becomes complete and we are joyfully *prayed through,* by a Seeking Life that flows through us into the world of human beings.

III

Worshiping in the light we become new creatures, making wholly new and astonishing responses to the entire outer setting of life. These responses are not reasoned out. They are, in large measure, spontaneous reactions of felt incompatibility between "the world's" judgments of value and the Supreme Value we adore deep in the Center. There is a total Instruction as well as specific instructions from the Light within. The dynamic illumination from the deeper level is shed upon the judgments of the surface level, and lo, the "former things are passed away, behold, they are become new."

Paradoxically, this total Instruction proceeds in two opposing directions at once. We are torn loose from earthly attachments and ambitions—*contemptus mundi.* And we are quickened to a divine but painful concern for the world—*amor mundi.* He plucks the world out of our hearts, loosening the chains of attachment. And He hurls the world into our hearts, where we and He together carry it in infinitely tender love.

Positions of prominence, eminences of social recognition that we once meant to attain—how puny and trifling they become! Our old ambitions and heroic dreams—what years we have wasted in feeding our own insatiable self-pride, when only His will truly matters! Our wealth and property, security now and in old age—upon what broken reeds have we leaned, when He is "the rock of our heart, and our portion forever!"

Unless the willingness is present to be stripped of our last earthly dignity and hope, and yet still praise Him, we have no message in this our day of refugees, bodily and spiritual. Nor have we yielded to the monitions of the Inner Instructor.

HOLY OBEDIENCE

Out in front of us is the drama of individuals and of nations, seething, struggling, laboring, dying. Upon this tragic drama in these days our eyes are all set in anxious watchfulness and in prayer. But within the silences of human souls an eternal drama is ever being enacted, in these days as well as in others. And on the outcome of this inner drama rests, ultimately, the outer pageant of history. It is the drama of the Hound of Heaven baying relentlessly upon the track of human beings. It is the drama of the lost sheep wandering in the wilderness, restless and lonely, feebly searching, while over the hills comes the wiser Shepherd. For His is a shepherd's heart, and He is restless until He holds His sheep in His arms. It is the drama of the Eternal Father drawing the prodigal home unto Himself, where there is bread enough and to spare. It is the drama of the Double Search, as Rufus Jones calls it. And always its chief actor is—the Eternal God of Love.

It is to one strand in this inner drama, one scene, where the Shepherd has found His sheep, that I would direct you. It is the life of absolute and complete and holy obedience to the voice of the Shepherd. But ever throughout the account the accent will be laid upon God, God the initiator, God the aggressor, God the seeker, God the stirrer into life, God the ground of our obedience, God the giver of the power to become children of God.

I. THE NATURE OF HOLY OBEDIENCE

Meister Eckhart wrote, "There are plenty to follow our Lord halfway, but not the other half. They will give up possessions, friends, and honors, but it touches them too closely to disown themselves." It is just this astonishing life that is willing to follow Him the other half, sincerely to disown itself, this life that intends *complete* obedience, without *any* reservations, that I would propose to you in all humility, in all boldness, in all seriousness. I mean this literally, utterly, completely, and I mean it for you and for me—commit your lives in unreserved obedience to Him.

If you don't realize the revolutionary explosiveness of this proposal you don't understand what I mean. This is something wholly different from mild, conventional religion that, with respectable skirts held back by dainty fingers, anxiously tries to fish the world out of the mud hole of its own selfishness. Our churches, our meeting houses are full of such respectable and amiable people. We have plenty of Quakers to follow God the first half of the way. Many of us have become as mildly and as conventionally religious as were the church folk of three centuries ago, against whose mildness and mediocrity and passionlessness George Fox and his followers flung themselves with all the passion of a glorious and a new discovery and with all the energy of dedicated lives. In some, says William James, religion exists as a dull habit, in others as an acute fever. Religion as a dull habit is not that for which Christ lived and died. Jesus put this pointedly when He said, "Ye must be born again" (John 3:3), and Paul

knew it: "If any man is in Christ, he is a new crea-
ture" (2 Cor. 5:17).

II. GATEWAYS INTO HOLY OBEDIENCE

In considering one gateway into this life of holy obedience, let us dare to venture together into the inner
sanctuary of the soul, where God meets us in awful
immediacy.

Some people come into holy obedience through
the gateway of profound mystical experience. It is an
overwhelming experience to fall into the hands of the
living God, to be invaded to the depths of one's
being by His presence, to be, without warning,
wholly uprooted from all earth-born securities and
assurances, and to be blown by a tempest of unbe-
lievable power that leaves one's old proud self utterly,
utterly defenseless, until one cries, "All Thy waves
and Thy billows are gone over me" (Ps. 42:7). Then
is the soul swept into a Loving Center of ineffable
sweetness, where calm and unspeakable peace and
ravishing joy steal over one. And one knows now
why Pascal wrote, in the center of his greatest mo-

ment, the single word, "Fire." There stands the world of struggling, sinful, earth-blinded people and nations, of plants and animals and wheeling stars of heaven, all new, all lapped in the tender, persuading Love at the Center. There stand the saints of the ages, their hearts open to view, and lo, their hearts are our heart and their hearts are the heart of the Eternal One.

One emerges from such soul-shaking, Love-invaded times into more normal states of consciousness. But one knows ever after that the Eternal Lover of the world, the Hound of Heaven, is utterly, utterly real, and that life must henceforth be forever determined by that Real. Like Saint Augustine one asks not for greater certainty of God but only for more steadfastness in Him. There, beyond, in Him is the true Center, and we are reduced, as it were, to nothing, for He is all.

But in contrast to this passive route to complete obedience, most people must follow what Jean-Nicholas Grou calls the active way, wherein *we* must struggle and, like Jacob of old, wrestle with the angel until the morning dawns, the active way wherein the

will must be subjected bit by bit, piecemeal and pro-
gressively, to the divine Will.

But the first step to the obedience of the second
half is the flaming vision of the wonder of such a life,
a vision that comes occasionally to us all, through
biographies of the saints, through the journals of Fox
and early Friends, through a life lived before our eyes,
through a haunting verse of the Psalms—"Whom
have I in heaven but Thee? And there is none upon
earth that I desire beside Thee" (Ps. 73:25)—through
meditation upon the amazing life and death of Jesus,
through a flash of illumination or, in Fox's language, a
great opening.

Once having the vision, the second step to holy
obedience is this: Begin where you are. Obey *now*.
Use what little obedience you are capable of, even if
it be like a grain of mustard seed. Begin where you
are. Live this present moment, this present hour as
you now sit in your seats, in utter, utter submission
and openness toward Him. Listen outwardly to these
words, but within, behind the scenes, in the deeper
levels of your lives where you are all alone with God
the Loving Eternal One, keep up a silent prayer,

"Open thou my life. Guide my thoughts where I dare not let them go. But Thou darest. Thy will be done."

And the third step in holy obedience, or a counsel, is this: If you slip and stumble and forget God for an hour, and assert your old proud self, and rely upon your own clever wisdom, don't spend too much time in anguished regrets and self-accusations but begin again, just where you are.

Yet a fourth consideration in holy obedience is this: Don't grit your teeth and clench your fists and say, "I will! I will!" Relax. Take hands off. Submit yourself to God. Learn to live in the passive voice—a hard saying for Americans—and let life be willed through you. For "I will" spells not obedience.

III. HUMILITY AND HOLINESS

The fruits of holy obedience are many. But two are so closely linked together that they can scarcely be treated separately. They are the passion for personal holiness and the sense of utter humility. God inflames the soul with a craving for absolute purity. But He, in His glorious otherness, empties us of ourselves in order that He may become all.

Humility does not rest, in final count, upon bafflement and discouragement and self-disgust at our shabby lives, a browbeaten, dog-slinking attitude. It rests upon the disclosure of the consummate wonder of God, upon finding that only God counts, that all our own self-originated intentions are works of straw. And so in lowly humility we must stick close to the Root and count our own powers as nothing except as they are enslaved in His power.

But O how slick and weasel-like is self-pride! Our learnedness creeps into our sermons with a clever quotation that adds nothing to God's glory, but a bit to our own. Our cleverness in business competition earns as much self-flattery as does the possession of the money itself. Our desire to be known and approved by others, to have heads nod approvingly about us behind our backs and flattering murmurs that we can occasionally overhear, confirms the discernment in Alfred Adler's elevation of the superiority motive. Our status as "weighty Friends" gives us secret pleasures that we scarcely own to ourselves, yet thrive upon. Yes, even pride in our own humility is one of the devil's own tricks.

Explore the depths of humility, not with your intellects but with your lives, lived in prayer of humble obedience. And there you will find that humility is not merely a human virtue. For there is a humility that is in God Himself. Be ye humble as God is humble. For love and humility walk hand in hand, in God as well as in human beings.

But there is something about deepest humility that makes people bold. For utter obedience is self-forgetful obedience. No longer do we hesitate and shuffle and apologize because, say we, we are weak, lowly creatures and the world is a pack of snarling wolves among whom we are sent as sheep by the Shepherd (Matt. 10:16). I must confess that, on human judgment, the world tasks we face are appalling—well-nigh hopeless. Only the inner vision of God, only the God-blindedness of unreservedly dedicated souls, only the utterly humble ones can bow and break the raging pride of a power-mad world. But self-renunciation means God-possession, the being possessed by God. Out of utter humility and self-forgetfulness comes the thunder of the prophets, "Thus saith the Lord." High station and low are leveled before Him. Be not fooled by the world's power. Imposing institutions of war and imperialism and greed are wholly vulnerable, for they, and we, are forever in the hands of a conquering God. These are not cheap and hasty words. The high and noble adventures of faith can in our truest moments be seen as no adventures at all, but certainties. And if we live in complete humility in God we can smile in patient assurance as we work. Will you be wise enough and humble enough to be little fools of God? For who can finally stay His power? Who can resist His persuading love? Truly says Saint Augustine, "There is something in humility which raiseth the heart upward." And John Woolman says, "Now I find that in pure obedience the mind learns contentment, in appearing weak and foolish to the wisdom which is of the World; and in these lowly labors, they who stand in a low place, rightly exercised under the Cross, will find nourishment."

Boldly must we risk the dangers that lie along the margins of excess, if we would live the life of the second half. For the life of obedience is a holy life, a separated life, a renounced life, cut off from worldly compromises, distinct, heaven-dedicated in the midst of other people, stainless as the snows upon the mountaintops.

They who walk in obedience, following God the second half, living the life of inner prayer of submission and exultation, on them God's holiness takes hold as a mastering passion of life. Yet ever they cry out in abysmal sincerity, "I am the blackest of all the sinners of the earth. I am a man of unclean lips, for mine eyes have seen the King, Jehovah of Hosts." For humility and holiness are twins in the astonishing birth of obedience in the human heart. So God draws unworthy us, in loving tenderness, up into fellowship with His glorious self.

IV. ENTRANCE INTO SUFFERING

Another fruit of holy obedience is entrance into suffering. I would not magnify joy and rapture, although they are unspeakably great in the committed life, for joy and rapture need no advocates. But we shrink from suffering and can easily call all suffering an evil thing. Yet we live in an epoch of tragic sorrows, when human beings are adding to the crueler forces of nature such blasphemous horrors as drag soul as well as body into hell. And holy obedience must walk in this world, not aloof and preoccupied, but stained with sorrow's travail.

Nor is the God-blinded soul given blissful oblivion but, rather, excruciatingly sensitive eyesight toward the human world. The sources of suffering for the tendered soul are infinitely multiplied, well-nigh beyond all endurance. Ponder this paradox in religious experience: "Nothing matters; everything matters." I recently had an unforgettable hour with a Hindu monk. He knew the secret of this paradox that we discussed together: "Nothing matters; everything matters." It is a key of entrance into suffering. He who knows only one half of the paradox can never enter that door of mystery and survive.

An awful solemnity is upon the earth, for the *last vestige* of earthly security is gone. *It has always been gone,* and religion has always said so, but we haven't believed it.

The Cross as dogma is painless speculation; the Cross as lived suffering is anguish and glory. Yet God, out of the pattern of His own heart, has planted the Cross along the road of holy obedience. And He enacts in the hearts of those He loves the miracle of willingness to welcome suffering and to know it for what it is—the final seal of His gracious love. I dare not urge you to your Cross. But He, more powerfully, speaks within you and me, to our truest selves, in our truest moments, and disquiets us with the world's needs. By inner persuasions He draws us to a few very definite tasks, *our* tasks, God's burdened heart particularizing His burdens in us. And He gives us the royal blindness of faith, and the seeing eye of the sensitized soul, and the grace of unflinching obedience. Then we see that nothing matters, and that everything matters, and that this my task matters for me and for my fellow human beings and for Eternity. And if we be utterly humble we may be given strength to be obedient even unto death, yea the death of the Cross.

In my deepest heart I know that some of us have to face our comfortable, self-oriented lives all over again. The times are too tragic, God's sorrow is too great, the human night is too dark, the Cross is too glorious for us to live as we have lived, in anything short of holy obedience. It may or it may not mean change in geography, in profession, in wealth, in earthly security. It does mean this: Some of us will have to enter upon a vow of renunciation and of dedication to the "Eternal Internal" that is as complete and as irrevocable as was the vow of the monk of the Middle Ages. Little groups of such utterly dedicated souls, knowing one another in Divine Fellowship, must take an irrevocable vow to live in this world yet not of this world.

V. SIMPLICITY

The last fruit of holy obedience is the simplicity of the trusting child, the simplicity of the children of God. It is the simplicity that lies beyond complexity. It is the naïveté that is the yonder side of sophistication. It is the beginning of spiritual maturity, which comes after the awkward age of religious busyness for the Kingdom of God—yet how many are caught, and arrested in development, within this adolescent development of the soul's growth! The mark of this simplified life is radiant joy. It lives in the Fellowship of the Transfigured Face. Knowing sorrow to the depths, it does not agonize and fret and strain, but in serene, unhurried calm it walks in time with the joy and assurance of Eternity. Knowing fully the complexity of human problems, it cuts through to the Love of God and ever cleaves to Him. Like the mercy of Shakespeare, "'tis mightiest in the mightiest." But it binds all obedient souls together in the fellowship of humility and simple adoration of Him who is all in all.

I have in mind something deeper than the simplification of our external programs, our absurdly crowded calendars of appointments through which so many pantingly and frantically gasp. These do become simplified in holy obedience, and the poise and peace we have been missing can really be found. But there is a deeper, an internal simplification of the whole of one's personality, stilled, tranquil, in childlike trust listening ever to Eternity's whisper, walking with a smile into the dark.

This amazing simplification comes when we "center down," when life is lived with singleness of eye, from a holy Center where the breath and stillness of Eternity are heavy upon us and we are wholly yielded to Him. Some of you know this holy, re-creating Center of eternal peace and joy and live in it day and night. Some of you may see it over the margin and wistfully long to slip into that amazing Center where the soul is at home with God. Be very faithful to that wistful longing. It is the Eternal Goodness calling you to return Home, to feed upon green pastures and walk beside still waters and live in the peace of the Shepherd's presence. It is the life *beyond* fevered strain. We are called beyond strain, to peace and power and joy and love and thorough abandonment of self. We are called to put our hands trustingly in His hand and walk the holy way, in no anxiety assuredly resting in Him.

THE BLESSED COMMUNITY

When we are drowned in the overwhelming seas of the love of God, we find ourselves in a new and particular relation to a few of our fellow human beings. The relation is so surprising and so rich that we despair of finding a word glorious enough and weighty enough to name it. The word *Fellowship* is discovered, but the word is pale and thin in comparison with the rich volume and luminous bulk and warmth of the experience that it would designate. For a new kind of life-sharing and of love has arisen of which we had had only dim hints before. Are these the bonds of love that knit together the early Christians, the very warp and woof of the Kingdom of God? In glad amazement and wonder we enter upon a relationship that we had not known the world contained for us. Why should such bounty be given to unworthy people like ourselves?

By no means is every one of our friends seen in this new and special light. A wholly new alignment of our personal relations appears. Some men and women whom we have never known before, or whom we have noticed only as a dim background for our more special friendships, suddenly loom large, step forward in our attention as men and women whom we now know to the depths. Our earlier conversations with these persons may have been few and brief, but now we know them, as it were, from within. For we discern that their lives are already down within that Center which has found us. And we hunger for their fellowship, with a profound, insistent craving that will not be denied.

Other acquaintances recede in significance; we know now that our relationships with them have always been nearer the surface of life. Many years of happy comradeship and common adventures we may have had together, but now we know that, at bottom, we have never been together in the deep silences of the Center, and that we never can be together there where the light of Eternity shines still and bright. For until they, too, have become wholly God-enthralled,

Light-centered, they can be only good acquaintances with whom we pass the time of day.

Not only do our daily friendships become re-aligned, our religious friends are also seen anew. Many impressions of worth are confirmed; others are reversed. Some of the most active church leaders, well known for their executive efficiency, people we have always admired, are shown, in the X-ray light of Eternity, to be agitated, half-committed, wistful, self-placating seekers, to whom the poise and serenity of the Everlasting have never come. The inexhaustible self-giving of others of our religious acquaintances we now understand, for the Eternal Love kindles an ardent and persistent readiness to do all things for, as well as through, Christ who strengthens us. In some we regret a well-intentioned but feverish overbusy-ness, not completely grounded in the depths of peace, and we wish they would not blur the beauty of their souls by fast motion. Others, who may not have been effective speakers or weighty financiers or charming conversationalists or members of prominent families, are found to be men and women on whom the dews of heaven have fallen indeed, who live continuously in the Center and who, in mature appreciation, understand our leaping heart and unbounded enthusiasm for God. And although they are not commissioned to any earthly office, yet they welcome us authoritatively into the Fellowship of Love. Every period of profound rediscovery of God's joyous immediacy is a period of emergence of this amazing group interknittedness of God-enthralled men and women who know one another *in Him*.

Yet still more astonishing is the Holy Fellowship, the Blessed Community, to those who are within it. Yet can one be surprised at being *at home?* In wonder and awe we find ourselves already interknit within unofficial groups of kindred souls. A "chance" conversation comes, and in a few moments we know that we have found and have been found by another member of the Blessed Community. Sometimes we are thus suddenly knit together in the bonds of a love far faster than those of many years' acquaintance. In unbounded eagerness we seek for more such fellowship, and wonder at the apparent lethargy of mere "members."

In the Fellowship cultural and educational and national and racial differences are leveled. Unlettered people are at ease with the truly humble scholar who lives in the Life, and the scholar listens with joy and openness to the precious experiences of God's dealing with working people. We find people with chilly theologies but with glowing hearts. We overleap the boundaries of church membership and find Lutherans and Roman Catholics, Jews and Christians, within the Fellowship. We reread the poets and the saints, and the Fellowship is enlarged. With urgent hunger we read the Scriptures, with no thought of pious exercise, but in order to find more friends for the soul. We brush past our historical learning in the Scriptures to seize upon those writers who lived in the Center, in the Life and in the Power. Particularly does devotional literature become illuminated, for the *Imitation of Christ,* and Augustine's *Confessions,* and Brother Lawrence's *Practice of the Presence of God* speak the language of the souls who live at the Center. Time telescopes and vanishes; centuries and creeds are overleaped. The incident of death puts no boundaries to the Blessed Community, wherein people live and love and work and pray in that Life and Power that gave forth the Scriptures. And we wonder and grieve at the overwhelmingly heady preoccupation of religious people with problems, problems, unless they have first come into the Fellowship of the Light.

The final grounds of holy Fellowship are in God. Lives immersed and drowned in God are drowned in love, and know one another in Him, and know one another in love. God is the medium, the matrix, the focus, the solvent. As Meister Eckhart suggests, one who is wholly surrounded by God, enveloped by God, clothed with God, glowing in selfless love toward Him—such a person no one can touch except he or she touch God also. Such lives have a common meeting point; they live in a common joyous enslavement. They go back into a single Center where they are at home with Him and with one another. It is as if every soul had a final base, and that final base of every soul is one single Holy Ground, shared in by all. Persons in the Fellowship are related to one another through Him, as all mountains go down into the same earth. They get at one another through Him. He is actively moving in all, coordinating those who are pliant to His will and suffusing them all with His glory and His joy.

The relation of each to all, through God, is real, objective, existential. It is an eternal relationship that is shared in by every stick and stone and bird and beast and saint and sinner of the universe. On all, the wooing love of God falls urgently, persuadingly. But those who, having will, yield to the loving urgency of that Life that knocks at their hearts are entered and possessed and transformed and transfigured. The scales fall from their eyes when they are given to eat of the tree of knowledge, the fruit of which is indeed for the healing of the nations, and they know themselves and their fellows as comrades in Eden, where God walks with them in the cool of the day. As there is a mysterious many-ing of God as He pours Himself forth into the universe, so there is a one-ing of those souls who find their way back to Him who is their home. And these are in the Holy Fellowship, the Blessed Community, of whom God is the head.

Within the wider Fellowship emerges the special circle of a few on whom, for each of us, a particular emphasis of nearness has fallen. These are our special gift and task. These we "carry" by inward, wordless prayer. Two people, three people, ten people may be in living touch with one another through Him who underlies their separate lives. This is an astounding experience, which I can only describe but cannot explain in the language of science. But in vivid experience of divine Fellowship, it is there. We know that these souls are with us, lifting their lives and ours continuously to God and opening themselves, with us, in steady and humble obedience to Him. It is as if the boundaries of our self were enlarged, as if we were within them and as if they were within us. Their strength, given to them by God, becomes our strength, and our joy, given to us by God, becomes their joy. In confidence and love we live together in Him. On the borders of the experience lie amazing events, at which reputable psychologists scoff, and for which I would not try any accounting. But the solid kernel of community of life in God is in the center of the experience, renewing our life and courage and commitment and love. For daily and hourly the cosmic Sacrament is enacted, the Bread and the Wine are divided amongst us by a heavenly Ministrant, and the substance of His body becomes our life and the substance of His blood flows in our veins. Holy is the Fellowship, wondrous is the Ministrant, marvelous is the Grail.

THE ETERNAL NOW
AND SOCIAL CONCERN

There is an experience of the Eternal breaking into time, which transforms all life into a miracle of faith and action. Unspeakable, profound, and full of glory as an inward experience, it is the root of concern for all creation, the true ground of social endeavor. This inward Life and the outward Concern are truly one whole and, were it possible, ought to be described simultaneously. But linear sequence and succession of words is our inevitable lot and compels us to treat separately what is not separate: first, the Eternal Now and the Temporal Now, and second, the nature and ground of Social Concern.

I. THE ETERNAL NOW AND THE TEMPORAL NOW

There is a tendency today, in this generation, to suppose that the religious life must prove its worth because it changes the social order. The test of the importance of any supposed dealing with Eternity is the benefits it may possibly bring to affairs in time. Time, and the enrichment of events in time, is supposed to pass a judgment upon the worth of fellowship with the Eternal. We breathe the air of a generation that, as the old phrase goes, "takes time seriously." People nowadays take time far more seriously than eternity.

German theology of a century ago emphasized a useful distinction between This-sidedness and Other-sidedness, or Here and Yonder. The church used to be chiefly concerned with Yonder; it was oriented toward the world beyond, and was little concerned with this world and its sorrows and hungers. Because the sincere working person, who suffered under economic privations, called out for bread, for whole-wheat-flour bread, the church of that day replied, "You're worldly-minded, you're crass, you're materialistic, you're oriented toward the Here. You ought to seek the heavenly, the eternal, the Yonder." But working people weren't materialistic, they were hungry; and Marxian socialism promised them just the temporal bread they needed, whereas the church had rebuked them for not hungering for the eternal Bread.

All this is now changed. We are in an era of This-sidedness, with a passionate anxiety about economics and political organization. And the church itself has largely gone "this-sided," and large areas of the Society of Friends seem to be predominantly concerned with this world, with time, and with the temporal order. And the test of the worthwhileness of any experience of Eternity has become, "Does it change things in time? If so, let us keep it; if not, let us discard it."

I submit that this is a lamentable reversal of the true order of dependence. Time is no judge of Eternity. It is the Eternal who is the judge and tester of time.

Once discover this glorious secret, this new dimension of life, and we no longer live merely in time but we live also in the Eternal. The world of time is no longer the sole reality of which we are aware. A second Reality hovers, quickens, quivers, stirs, energizes us, breaks in upon us and in love embraces us, together with all things, within Himself. We live our lives at two levels simultaneously, the level of time and the level of the Timeless. They form one sequence, with a fluctuating border between them. Sometimes the glorious Eternal is in the ascendancy, but still we are aware of our daily temporal routine. Sometimes the clouds settle low and we are chiefly in the world of time, yet we are haunted by a smaller sense of Presence, in the margin of consciousness.

But, fluctuating in predominance though the two levels be, such a discovery of an Eternal Life and Love breaking in, nay, always there, but we were too preoccupied to notice it, makes life glorious and new. And one sings inexpressibly sweet songs within oneself, and one *tries* to keep one's inner hilarity and exuberance within bounds lest, like the disciples at Pentecost, we be mistaken for people filled with new wine.

But now let us examine the ordinary experience of time, unrevised by this great discovery of the Eternal Life springing up within it. Ordinary people, busy earning a living, exercise care, caution, foresight. They calculate probabilities. They study the past in order to predict and control the future. Then when they have weighed all the factors and plotted the outcome, with energy and industry they will themselves into persistent activity along the lines of calculated wisdom.

And much religious work is carried on in just this same way. With shrewd and canny foresight, religious people study the past, examine all the factors in the situation that they can foresee, and then decide what is wisest to undertake, or what is most congruous with the Christian life described in the Gospels. Then they breathe a prayer to God to reinforce their wills and keep them strong in executing their resolve.

In this process, time spreads itself out like a ribbon, stretching away from the *now* into the past, and forward from the *now* into the future, at the far end of which stands the New Jerusalem. In this ribbon of time we live, anxiously surveying the past in order to learn how to manage the most important part of the ribbon, the future.

The experience of Divine Presence changes all this familiar picture. There come times when the Presence *steals upon us,* all unexpected not the product of agonized effort, and we live in a new dimension of life. You who have experienced such plateaus of glory know what I mean. Out from the plain of daily living suddenly loom such plateaus. Before we know it we are walking upon their heights, and all the old familiar landscape becomes new. The experience of Paul is very true: "The former things are passed away; behold, they are become new." One walks in the world yet above the world as well, giddy with the height, with feather tread, with effortlessness and calm security, meeting the daily routine, yet never losing the sense of Presence. Sometimes these periods are acute and brief, too dazzling to report to anyone. Sometimes they are less elevated but more prolonged, with a milder sense of glory and of lift, yet as surely of a piece with the more acute experience. Such experiences are emotionless, in themselves, but suffuse all emotion with a background of peace, utter, utter peace and security.

Instead of being the active, hurrying church worker and the anxious, careful planner of shrewd moves toward the good life, we become pliant creatures, less brittle, less obstinately rational. The energizing, dynamic center is not in us but in the Divine Presence in which we share. Religion is not *our* concern; it is God's concern. The sooner we stop thinking *we* are the energetic operators of religion and discover that God is at work, as the Aggressor, the Invader, the Initiator, so much the sooner do we discover that our task is to call people to *be still and know,* listen, hearken in quiet invitation to the subtle promptings of the Divine. Our task is to encourage others first to let go, to cease striving, to give over this fevered effort of the self-sufficient religionist trying to please an external deity. Count on God knocking on the doors of time. God is the Seeker, and not we alone; He is anxious to swell out our time-nows into an Eternal Now by filling them with a sense of Presence. I am persuaded that religious people do not with sufficient seriousness count on God as an active factor in the affairs of the world. "Behold, I stand at the door and knock," but too many well-intentioned people are so preoccupied with the clatter of effort to do something *for* God that they don't hear Him asking that He might do something *through* them.

An invariable element in the experience of Now is that of unspeakable and exquisite joy, peace, serene release. A new song is put into our mouths. It is not we who sing; it is the Eternal Song of the Other, who sings in us, who sings unto us, and through us into the world.

For the Eternal is urgently, actively breaking into time, working through those who are willing *to be laid hold upon,* to surrender *self*-confidence and *self*-centered effort, that is, self-originated effort, and let the Eternal be the dynamic guide in re-creating, through us, our time-world.

This is the first fruit of the Spirit—a joy unspeakable and full of glory.

The second is love. It is second not in importance but merely in order of mentioning. For it is true that in the experience of Divine Presence that which flows over the ocean of darkness is an infinite ocean of light and *love.* In the Eternal Now all human beings become seen in a new way. We enfold them in our love, and we and they are enfolded together within the great Love of God as we know it in Christ. Once walk in the Now and people are changed, in our sight, as we see them from the plateau heights. They aren't just masses of struggling beings, furthering or thwarting our ambitions, or, in far larger numbers, utterly alien to and insulated from us. We become identified with them and suffer when they suffer and rejoice when they rejoice. One might almost say we become cosmic mothers, tenderly caring for all. But that, I believe, is experienced only in the acutest stages of mystic ecstasy, whereas I have been discussing the experience of milder, less lofty plateaus of glory, prolonged days and even weeks of sense of Presence wherein, as Isaac Penington would say, the springings of the Life are ever fresh. In such a sense of Presence there is a vast background of cosmic Love and tender care for all things (plants included, I find for myself), but in the foreground arise special objects of love and concern and tender responsibility. The people we know best, see oftenest, have most to do with, these are *reloved* in a new and a deeper way.

Heaven's eternal Now within us makes us speak blasphemous things, for we seem to assume the prerogatives of God. But this is a part of that astounding boldness of which I mean to speak under the head of peace—our next main fruit of the spirit. For those who have been brought back to the *Principle* within them are exquisitely drawn toward all others who have found the same Principle.

The third element in the experience of Presence, after love and joy, is peace. Strain! Strain! Out of such attitudes are built those lives that get written up in the success stories of the *American Magazine*. And religious people think they must work hard and please God and make a good record and bring in the kingdom! Has the Nietzschean ideal of the superman, with heroic, world-striding power, hypnotized the church into an overactivistic attitude?

And then comes the sense of Presence. The Eternal Now breaks through the time-nows, and all is secure. A sense of absolute security and assurance of being linked with an overcoming Power replaces the old anxieties about the Kingdom. One who knows the Presence knows peace, and one who knows peace knows power and walks in complete faith that that objective Power and Love that has overtaken him or her will overcome the world.

Submit yourself to the Eternal Now, and in peace serene, in the boldness of perfect faith, you can advance into miraculous living. Or, in the opposite direction, our time-now may say, "Do this. You are well prepared for it. Your education and training fit you, perhaps to teach, to preach, to counsel, to guide an enterprise. And if you don't, nobody will." But the Eternal Now in us may say, "Stay. Wait. Don't rely upon yourself. Don't think you can reason yourself into your obligation. Know you not that I can raise up of these stones people better able than you to do this?"

Thus in faith we go forward, with breathtaking boldness, and in faith we stand still, unshaken, with amazing confidence. For the time-nows are rooted in the Eternal Now, which is a steadfast Presence, an infinite ocean of light and love that is flowing over the ocean of darkness and death.

2. THE NATURE AND GROUND OF SOCIAL CONCERN

The experience of Divine Presence wholly satisfies, and there are a few who, like those on the Mount of Transfiguration, want to linger there forever and never return to the valleys where people live, where there are demons to be cast out. But there is more to the experience of God than that of being plucked out of the world. The fuller experience, I am sure, is of a Love that sends us out into the world.

There is a tendering of the soul toward *everything* in creation, from the sparrow's fall to the slave under the lash. The hard-lined face of a money-bitten financier is as deeply touching to the *tendered* soul as are the burned-out eyes of miners' children, remote and unseen victims of his so-called success. There is a sense in which, in this terrible tenderness, we become one with God and bear in our quivering souls the sins and burdens, the benightedness and the tragedy of the creatures of the whole world, and suffer in their suffering, and die in their death.

There are two ways in which a concern is a particularization. It is a particularization of the Divine Concern of God for all creation. But it is a particularization of *my* responsibility also, in a world too vast and a lifetime too short for me to carry all responsibilities. My cosmic love, or the Divine Lover loving within me, cannot accomplish its full intent, *which is universal saviorhood,* within the limits of threescore years and ten. But the Loving Presence does not burden us equally with all things, but considerately puts upon

each of us just a few central tasks, as emphatic responsibilities. For each of us these special undertakings are
our share in the joyous burdens of love. We cannot
die on *every* cross, nor are we expected to.

THE SIMPLIFICATION OF LIFE

The problem we face today needs very little time for its statement. Our lives in a modern city grow too complex and overcrowded. Even the necessary obligations that we feel we must meet grow overnight, like Jack's beanstalk, and before we know it we are bowed down with burdens, crushed under committees, strained, breathless, and hurried, panting through a never-ending program of appointments. We are too busy to be good wives to our husbands, good homemakers, good companions of our children, good friends to our friends, and with no time at all to be friends to the friendless. But if we withdraw from public engagements and interests in order to spend quiet hours with the family, the guilty calls of citizenship whisper disquieting claims in our ears. Our children's schools should receive our interest; the civic problems of our community need our attention; the wider issues of the nation and of the world are heavy upon us. Our professional status, our social obligations, our membership in this or that very important organization put claims upon us. And in frantic fidelity we try to meet at least the necessary minimum of calls upon us. But we're weary and breathless. And we know and regret that our life is slipping away, with our having tasted so little of the peace and joy and serenity we are persuaded it should yield to a soul of wide caliber. The times for the deeps of the silences of the heart seem so few.

Let me first suggest that we are giving a false explanation of the complexity of our lives. We blame it upon the complex environment. Our complex living, we say, is due to the complex world we live in, with its radios and autos, which give us more stimulation per square hour than used to be given per square day to our grandmothers.

We Western peoples are apt to think our great problems are external, environmental. We are not skilled in the inner life, where the real roots of our problem lie. For I would suggest that the true explanation of the complexity of our program is an inner one, not an outer one. The outer distractions of our interests reflect an inner lack of integration of our own lives. We are trying to be several selves at once, without all our selves being organized by a single, mastering Life within us. Each of us tends to be, not a single self, but a whole committee of selves. There is the civic self, the parental self, the financial self, the religious self, the society self, the professional self, the literary self. And each of our selves is in turn a rank individualist, not cooperative but shouting out its vote loudly for itself when the voting time comes. And all too commonly we follow the common American method of getting a quick decision among conflicting claims within us. It is as if we have a chairman of our committee of the many selves within us who does not integrate the many into one but merely counts the votes at each decision and leaves disgruntled minorities.

We feel honestly the pull of many obligations and try to fulfill them all. And we are unhappy, uneasy, strained, oppressed, and fearful we shall be shallow. For over the margins of life comes a whisper, a faint call, a premonition of richer living that we know we are passing by. Strained by the very mad pace of our daily outer burdens, we are further strained by an inward uneasiness, because we have hints that there is a way of life vastly richer and deeper than all this hurried existence, a life of unhurried serenity and peace and power. If only we could slip over into that Center! If only we could find the Silence that is the source of sound! We have seen and known some people who seem to have found this deep Center of living, where the fretful calls of life are integrated, where no as well as yes can be said with confidence. We've seen such lives, integrated, unworried by the tangles of close decisions, unhurried, cheery, fresh, positive. These are not people of dallying idleness nor of obviously mooning meditation; they are busy carrying their full load as well as we, but without any chafing of the shoulders with the burden, with quiet joy and springing step. Surrounding the trifles of their daily life is an aura of infinite peace and power and joy. We are so strained and tense, with our burdened lives; they are so poised and at peace.

There is a divine Abyss within us all, a holy Infinite Center, a Heart, a Life who speaks in us and through us to the world. We have all heard this holy Whisper at times. At times we have followed the Whisper, and amazing equilibrium of life, amazing effectiveness of living set in. But too many of us have heeded the Voice only at times. Only at times have we submitted to His holy guidance. We have not counted this Holy Thing within us to be the most precious thing in the world.

And under the silent, watchful eye of the Holy One we all are standing, whether we know it or not. And in that Center, in that holy Abyss where the Eternal dwells at the base of our being, our programs, our gifts to Him, our offerings of duties performed are again and again revised in their values. Many of the things we are doing seem so important to us. We haven't been able to say no to them, because they seemed so important. But if we *center down,* as the old phrase goes, and live in that holy Silence that is dearer than life, and take our life program into the silent places of the heart, with complete openness, ready to do, ready to renounce according to His leading, then many of the things we are doing lose their vitality for us.

Do you really want to live your lives, every moment of your lives, in His Presence? Do you long for Him, crave Him? Do you love His Presence? Does every drop of blood in your body love Him? Does every breath you draw breathe a prayer, a praise to Him? Do you sing and dance within yourselves, as you glory in His love?

We have too long been prim and restrained. The fires of the love of God, of our love toward God, and of His love toward us, are very hot. "Thou shalt love the Lord thy God with all thy heart and soul and mind and strength." Do we really do it? Is love steadfastly directed toward God, in our minds, all day long? Do we intersperse our work with gentle prayers and praises to Him? Do we live in the steady peace of God, a peace down at the very depths of our souls, where all strain is gone and God is already victor over the world, already victor over our weaknesses? This life, this abiding, enduring peace that never fails, this serene power and unhurried conquest, inward conquest over ourselves, outward conquest over the world, is meant to be ours. It is a life that is freed from strain and anxiety and hurry, for something of the Cosmic Patience of God becomes ours. Are our lives *unshakable,* because we are clear down on bedrock, rooted and grounded in the love of God? This is the first and the great commandment.

Do you *want* to live in such an amazing divine Presence that life is transformed and transfigured and transmuted into peace and power and glory and miracle? If you do, then you can. For, except for spells of sickness in the family and when the children are small, when terrific pressure comes upon us, we find time for what we *really want* to do.

I find that a life of little whispered words of adoration, of praise, of prayer, of worship can be breathed all through the day. One can have a very busy day, outwardly speaking, and yet be steadily in the holy Presence. We do need a half hour or an hour of quiet reading and relaxation. But I find that one can carry the re-creating silences within oneself *well-nigh all the time*.

I think it is clear that I am talking about a revolutionary way of living. Religion isn't something to be added to our other duties and thus make our lives yet more complex. The life with God is the center of life, and all else is remodeled and integrated by it. It gives the singleness of eye. The most important thing is not to be perpetually passing out cups of cold water to a thirsty world. We can get so fearfully busy trying to carry out the second great commandment, "Thou shalt love thy neighbor as thyself," that we are underdeveloped in our devoted love to God. But we must love God as well as neighbor. These things ye ought to have done and not to have left the other only partially done.

There is a way of life so hid with Christ in God that in the midst of the day's business one is inwardly lifting brief prayers, short ejaculations of praise, subdued whispers of adoration and of tender love to the Beyond that is within. No one need know about it. I only speak to you because it is a sacred trust, not mine but to be given to others. One can live in a well-nigh continuous state of unworded prayer, directed toward God, directed toward people and enterprises we have on our heart. There is no hurry about it all; it is a life unspeakable and full of glory, an inner world of splendor within which we, unworthy, may live. Some of you know it and live in it; others of you may wistfully long for it; it can be yours.

Now out from such a holy Center come the commissions of life. Our fellowship with God issues in world concern. We cannot keep the love of God to ourselves. It spills over. It quickens us. It makes us see the world's needs anew. We love people, and we grieve to see them blind when they might be seeing, asleep with all the world's comforts when they ought to be awake and living sacrificially, accepting the world's goods as their right when they really hold them only in temporary trust. It is because from this holy Center we relove people, relove our neighbors as ourselves, that we are bestirred to be means of their awakening. The deepest human need is not food and clothing and shelter, important as they are. It is God.

This love of people is well-nigh as amazing as the love of God. Do we want to help people because we feel sorry for them, or because we genuinely love them? The world needs something deeper than pity; it needs love. (How trite that sounds, how real it is!)

But in our love of people are we to be excitedly hurried, sweeping all individuals and tasks into our loving concern? No, that is God's function. But He, working within us, portions out His vast concern into bundles and lays on each of us our portion. These become our tasks. Life from the Center is a heaven-directed life. The Cosmic Patience becomes, in part, our patience, for after all God is at work in the world. It is not we alone who are at work in the world, frantically finishing a work to be offered to God.

Life from the Center is a life of unhurried peace and power. It is simple. It is serene. It is amazing. It is triumphant. It is radiant. It takes no time, but it occupies all our time. And it makes our life programs new and overcoming. We need not get frantic. He is at the helm. And when our little day is done, we lie down quietly in peace, for all is well.

ABOUT THOMAS KELLY

M uch of the information for this biographical sketch was taken from "A Biographical Memoir," by Douglas V. Steere, printed in the original volume of *A Testament of Devotion* published by Harper & Brothers in 1941.

Thomas Raymond Kelly was born on June 4, 1893, on a farm in southwestern Ohio. His father died when Thomas was four, and when Thomas was ten his mother moved the family to Wilmington, Ohio, so that he could attend the Quaker school, Wilmington College.

Kelly graduated from Wilmington in 1913 with a concentration in the physical sciences, spent an extra year at Haverford College, and then went on to teach science at Pickering College, a Quaker preparatory school in Canada. In the autumn of 1916 he entered Hartford Theological Seminary to prepare for religious work in the Far East.

Kelly's studies at Hartford were interrupted by America's entry into the war, and Kelly volunteered as a Quaker, first in canteen duty with the Y.M.C.A. and then in work with German prisoners of war in England. Returning to the States, Kelly took his Bachelor of Divinity degree at the Seminary in 1919.

Fellow alumni of the Seminary remember a fun-loving Kelly who was always to be found at the center of any goings-on. It was during these years that Thomas Kelly met Lael Macy. The two were married on the day after his graduation, and they returned to Wilmington College, where Kelly had been offered a position.

Kelly's interest in the Far East hadn't deserted him, and he returned to Hartford Theological Seminary to undertake a course in Eastern and Western philosophy. In June 1924 he was awarded his Ph.D.

In the postwar years of 1924–25, Thomas and Lael Kelly spent fifteen months in Berlin contributing to the Quaker effort. Wilbur K. Thomas, the executive secretary of the American Friends Service Committee in those years, writes, "The Center was in need of a strong, spiritual leader. Thomas R. Kelly was the man."

In September 1925, the couple moved to Richmond, Indiana, where Kelly taught philosophy at Earlham College. Kelly was anxious to raise philosophy to the place of high respect he felt it deserved in a liberal arts education. Kelly's closest friend at Earlham remembers him this way: "He was in rebellion against what seemed to him the churchliness or institutionalism of the self-consciously religious ... he wished to be a living witness of truth."

A daughter, Lois, was born to the Kellys in 1928, and in 1930 the family moved to Cambridge, Massachusetts, where Kelly studied philosophy at Harvard University. Kelly had hoped that the two years at Harvard might bring an opportunity for teaching philosophy in some university in the East, but the economic depression wore on, and in the spring of 1932 Kelly made the decision to return to Earlham College, where a position was being held open for him.

In the spring of 1935 Kelly took a position teaching philosophy at the University of Hawaii, where he enjoyed the opportunity to associate with Chinese and Japanese scholars and to teach various courses in

Eastern philosophy. A son, Richard Kelly, was born in Hawaii in February 1936. In March of that year Thomas Kelly joined the philosophy department at Haverford College, replacing D. Elton Trueblood, who had been called to be chaplain and professor of the philosophy of religion at Stanford University. The Kelly family arrived in Haverford early in September 1936 and found a comfortable place in the Quaker community there.

Kelly was happy at Haverford. While there he saw the publication of his *Explanation and Reality in the Philosophy of Emile Meyerson* in the fall of 1937, marking an end to seven years of intense scholarship. After this, Kelly seemed to undergo a marked and abrupt change. He was at last able to reconcile his commitment to science and reason with his belief in God. But there was more to change than just intellectual harmony.

The new direction his life began to take was precipitated by two events—one a crushing personal defeat and the other an immersion into suffering. It resulted in what a former student and close friend, T. Canby Jones, called " a second conversion."

The personal defeat came when he stood for his oral exams for a second Ph.D., this time at Harvard, and failed the exams miserably. For Kelly, to be denied a Harvard Ph.D. was catastrophic, and it drove him into a deep depression. Yet, within months, out of the ruins of personal failure, arose a new vision of God-intoxicated life.

This change was reinforced and advanced by a trip to Hitler's Germany in the summer of 1938. "I have never had such a soul-overturning summer or period as this," he wrote. What Kelly witnessed in his German friends was a depth of consecration, a simplicity of faith, and a baptism of suffering that deepened his own life. In those months Kelly says he learned "the real pain of suffering *with* people."

Many of the writings included in this volume grew out of this period. Most of them were printed in *The Friend,* a Quaker religious and literary journal published biweekly in Philadelphia. "The Eternal Now and Social Concern" appeared in March 1938; the Richard Cary Lecture, "The Light Within," was published in German in August 1938; the counsel on simplicity appeared in a symposium on that subject in

March 1939; "The Blessed Community" in September 1939. In late March 1939, Thomas Kelly delivered the annual William Penn Lecture, entitled "Holy Obedience," to the Yearly Meeting of Quakers.

In the years following this visit to Germany, Thomas Kelly continued to work with the American Friends Service Committee, helping to establish the Quaker Center at Shanghai and guiding a small committee that met to study the Eastern scene. He also became chairman of the Fellowship Council and as such served for two years on the Board of Directors of the Service Committee.

Thomas Kelly died suddenly of a heart attack on January 17, 1941, at the age of forty-seven. Kelly's friend from Earlham wrote this to Lael Kelly: "I cannot tell you adequately, and yet I think you know, how much I loved Tom. . . . He was the perfect friend, whether we shared the gay sunlight of humor, or ascended the peaks of highest vision together. . . . The thought of him was always a beatitude, a great light, a wind of courage."